Come in From the Cold

Michael Krutz

WestBow
PRESS
A DIVISION OF THOMAS NELSON

WestBow Press books may be ordered through booksellers or by contacting:

WestBow Press
A Division of Thomas Nelson
1663 Liberty Drive
Bloomington, IN 47403
www.westbowpress.com
1-(866) 928-1240

Because of the dynamic nature of the Internet, any web addresses or links contained in this book may have changed since publication and may no longer be valid. The views expressed in this work are solely those of the author and do not necessarily reflect the views of the publisher, and the publisher hereby disclaims any responsibility for them.

Any people depicted in stock imagery provided by Thinkstock are models, and such images are being used for illustrative purposes only.

Certain stock imagery © Thinkstock.

ISBN: 978-1-4497-4862-3 (sc)
ISBN: 978-1-4497-4861-6 (e)

Library of Congress Control Number: 2012907094

Printed in the United States of America

WestBow Press rev. date: 05/25/2012

Contents

Depression

Depression is not just a word it's a feeling and a terrible weight,
at times it seems it can consume your whole world.
Depression is real, it loves to break,
it will try to tear you down and break you, then chain you down
after your broken,
it will wake you up in the morning and tuck you in at night,
the pain is real and heavy, it will wear upon you
and wear upon you.
Depression's intentions are not to just wound but to destroy.
Rich or poor, Strong or weak, A well known name or a name no
one knows makes no difference.
No difference to color, language, height, weight or age,
only to break.
Depression will not take money or gifts to leave, it cares for
neither, you mean nothing to them.
To make your heart as cold as it can, to make your life as hard as
it can, only to break you,
then cast you to the side into the pile of ruins and wrecks.
They'll use money, they'll use poverty
They'll use beauty, they'll use no beauty
They'll use victories, they'll use failures, They'll use loved ones,
they'll use loneliness.
They'll use alcohol, they'll use drugs, They'll use broken dreams,
they'll use no dreams.
They don't care what they use.
Depression will make you feel like you are worthless,
nothing but one more number in a line of 80 million more
numbers of nothing . . .
THE words you have just read are not made up, they are real
words and real feelings from real time spent in the pits and
storms and valleys of this world.
But me i have never been alone, my Lord GOD has kept me
through the pain and the cold and the depression, through the
storms that would have crushed me.

Just as the feelings of the pain and depression are real so is the feeling of a living Love from the Living GOD and a Living CHRIST JESUS.

You never have to make believe with Them, if you want to make believe go someplace else.

THEIR ALMIGHTY POWER IS AS REAL AND TRUE AS THEIR ALL POWERFUL LOVE.

You don't have to break the chains yourself, even though you feel alone you are not alone.

Let The HOLY ONES break the chains.

COME IN FROM THE COLD.

Staring

When_i walk into the Light
That is not made by man's hands
I find myself staring at the ground
Because of the brilliance of Your Light
And because of what i am or what my heart convicts me of
what i should have been
I find myself staring at the ground
The way of man seemed more than the way of God
Pleasures, titles, lands & deeds
Money, fame and fortune
But here I am
But where am I?
How far did i come,
but how far did i really come?
How great was I
or
How far did i really fall?
How bright did i shine
or
did i shine at all?
The way of man might seem
more than the way of God
"but it cannot compare"
When i walk into
"Your Light"
I find myself staring at the ground

Behind The Painted Smile

Holy GOD You have a Holy SON how could You love
a boy like me?
Lord JESUS You are the Holy Son, GOD has sent
You to save a wretched boy like me.
They said You gave everything so we could live
with You and Him,
The Holy Ones, The Holy Ones, The Holy Ones.
So far away from peace i was so lost, so lost, so lost.
I'm born of flesh and lost my way but still a light shines round
about me, all around me everyday in this dark world, in this
cold world, in this lost world.
You lift me up upon Your Love, Upon Your Love You lift me up,
Upon Your Love, Your Holy Love, Your tender Love.
So if you are out there by yourself or in a crowd with many faces
all around you, or even in the midst of your own family and in
your heart you feel so lost, so alone, so lost, so alone.
I have had this feeling in my heart, i have felt this pain to in my
soul, i have been in this pit,
lost in this storm, this long lost valley. You are not alone in this
dark place, you are not alone in this hard place, you are not
alone in this bad place, you are not alone. Upon Their love
They'll lift you up, They will rescue you, They will lift you up,
They will break the chains that hold you down, They will set
your spirit free. So when you find yourself in these dire straits
and all around is sorrow, all roads lead in and there's no escape
and you can not see tomorrow, and time just goes on and on
and on, and the pain doesn't leave it just gets worse and you
can't believe after all this time it could just keep getting worse.
And you can't escape because there's no roads out, and you
feel so tired, so broken, so nothing and you feel like giving up.
This is what i used to do, "i'd put a smile on my face, i'd paint
it on my face each day, can't you see that all is fine when you
look into my eyes." Now if you look real close and listen real
hard you might be able to hear the cry from a person's heart

from behind a painted smile. You won't be able to hear the cry going 90 mph,you won't be able to hear the cry if you are not really listening, you won't be able to sense it if you are not really looking and you might not be able to even if you are. Who's Smile Did You See Today?

Hello, good morning, what's for dinner, see you next sunday. "What About The Smile"?

So if you are out there by yourself or in a crowd with many faces all around you or even in the midst of your own family and you feel so alone, so lost, so alone. Me, i'd put a smile on my face, i'd paint it on my face each day, can't you see that all is fine when you look into my eye's?

I don't think you will be hearing the person say "help me" i think it will sound more like "i'm o.k. or i'm fine," then maybe a quick changing of the subject. I do know you will have to look inside their heart and it might sound more like this, "more time has passed and i am yet deeper in this pit,have i reached the bottom yet, does anyone know i am even here, can't you see where i am, can't you hear my heart cry, can't you sense the pain." I do know you will have to look inside their heart and there's only one way to do that. HOLY GOD of LIGHT, HOLY GOD of POWER, HOLY GOD of MERCY, HOLY GOD of COMPASSION in JESUS Name.

It's time to lose the "painted smile" or look past one painted on someone else's face.

Can't YOU See That All Is Fine When You Look Into My Eye's?

Am I Great Now

And what is great?
That my words should be heard or that my name should be
known or the circles in which my name is mentioned, maybe it's
the many times they take my picture or shake my hand.
And what is great, tell me?
If i was a rich man and all favored me, if i was a prophet and
everyone called me prophet,or if i was the president and all
sought to be near me, is this great, am i great now?
If i wrote a famous book, if i made a famous movie, if i wrote a
well known paper, if i was a famous singer, am i great now? now
am i great? great is what?
Great is what, what if i'm sad all the time.
Great is what, what if i'm poor, hungry and broken.
Great is what, what if i'm so tired and i feel like giving up and i
just can't go on anymore.
Great is what, what if my heart cries tears quietly so
no one can see or hear.
Am i great now? "Can your heart see me as great now"?
What is great? I know in my heart what it is.
It's to be Blessed with the Love of The HOLY ONES.
A Living GOD and A Living CHRIST JESUS.
With a penny or many dollars, with a sad heart or a happy one,
with a song on your heart or even when your heart is too heavy
to sing, when you are scared and so very tired.
The Love of Heaven Will Hold You.
What is great? THEIR LOVE ALONE IS GREAT.

Gifts

Why do you love me, let me count the ways,
i can't think of any, my mind is empty, my heart is searching, i
can't think of any.
Isn't it funny or maybe it's just sad, happy / sad,
when i'm happy the days are easier, when i'm sad the
days are harder,
why aren't more of the days easier?
There's a lot of people who are used to hard and still hope in
You, there's a lot of people who smile all the time and still need
to know You, a smile without You, it sounds so strange.
How can You love us, let me count the ways,
my mind is empty, my heart is searching, let me see the way.
There's a lot of people who are used to hard and the hard has
made their hearts hard,
there's a lot of people who smile all the time and they can only
smile because of You.
I think about gifts, why do You love me, let me know the way.
ONE GIFT, ONE WAY, "LORD JESUS."
I think about gifts, i think about You,
so i got lost in my mind and i needed to know more about gifts
and i wanted to know everything from the very
best so i asked GOD.
I didn't know if He would answer me but i knew He would.
I asked Him about gifts and He told me; there was a time when
His mind was empty, His heart was sad, He just didn't know,
then He said "I gave from My heart everything I loved, My
greatest gift wherein no gifts compare, MY SON JESUS."
And my mind got lost in Their Love.

Your Love is Constant

Gifts of gold that caught my eye, fame and fortune stood close
by, gifts and pleasures all were free and my heart followed my
eye or did my eye follow my heart when all the world's treasures
came close by. They brought me a mirror and with many words
told me of my beauty and my great worth along with all of the
many gifts and my heart felt like it had been "found". It was like
a dream, a dream starring me, gifts for me, look at me.
Then the light changed as does time and i looked so many are
broken this caught my eye, sorrow and pain stood close by,
when would the pain end i did not know, and my heart followed
my eye or did my eye follow my heart when all the world's
sorrow came close by. I don't want a mirror, don't bring me one,
i don't want to look, my heart feels lost, it's like a dream,
a bad dream starring me.
I fight with everything i fail too often, sometimes i feel so bad
inside but You never left my side.
My candle that is my heart it needs help, it grows dim but You
still hold me and not by accident or for a short time, so if it was
not by accident that You made me and that You hold me always,
i know You will see me through this storm. I believe it to be
true, i know this to be true, as true as Your love.
Down this long lost road though this valley when i grew weaker
Your strength increased for me.
When my heart cried tears of sorrow Your tender love drew me
closer. When my heart cried out in anguish Your sweet sweet
sweet tender mercies covered me. Your love is constant, holding
me always, causing me to breath, taking away the heaviness
of my heart and mind.
When my heart is up high in the heavens or down low in the
valleys Your love is constant, making sense in my life when
nothing else makes sense. You wipe away my tears and give me
hope. There is a tomorrow with You and the joy of
forever with You.

Your love causes my heart to feel like it has a song to sing, a
purpose, a reason for being.
It gives me soundness in a shaking world.
Your loving kindness and Your loving favor are
light unto my soul.
Thank You Father in Heaven and Lord Jesus Christ
for not giving up on me.
Keeping a place of Mercy for me always in Your Heart.

Surrounded

I find myself surrounded by Their love, if Their love was as the
ocean i'd find myself in the midst of it, all so fully surrounded,
surrounded by Their strength and softness,
so loved and blessed and held.
My heart does not need fantasies, my heart does not need false
hope,and in my life i just don't need "make beliefs or make
believes," all these can lead to depression,
sorrow or even worse "doubt."
And i don't need anymore chains, i'm already familiar with the
pits, the storms and the valleys of this life, but the Lord has kept
me through it all even when i couldn't love myself or even cared
what happened anymore. They still shined Their love upon my
heart, into my life.
They kept looking out for me with a real love, not a make
believe love and not a love that gives false hope. Their love is
a real love, a love that never gives up, a love you can sense, a
love you can taste, a love you can really feel, a love that really
holds Their babes. And you wonder what you could have done
to receive a precious,so precious love. A love so slow to judge
and tender in touch, a love of sweetness of fragrance, a love of
richness of color, a love of beauty and flavor wherein there is no
compare, a love of exalted compassion. And in your mind you
know there's nothing you could have done to earn or deserve to
have this Holiness poured upon you.
I find myself surrounded by Their love, if Their love was as the
ocean i'd find myself in the midst of it, all so fully surrounded,
surrounded by Their strength and softness,
so loved and blessed and held.

Your Smile

GOD if You can hear me, if You are there,
they said creation is supposed to be about life, "a celebration",
well, it was another hard day today, with a song on my heart or
often a sigh You still hold me.
Your love can still make a tired person feel young again, despite
the many miles in the mud and heat. You kept me in Your love
and did not choose to hate me.
In this world the people don't need to be taught about hate,
sorrow, pain and suffering, they already know. They don't have
to be taught about bills they can't pay, they don't have to be
taught about shattered dreams or broken marriages or burying
loved ones, they already know, its been another hard day today,
thank you for your smile.
There's those who would have the people to be damned but
You did not damn us.
You smiled that smile towards us, in a world of many smiles
there's none like Yours.
In Your smile there is a song, i can tell, it's a beautiful song, as
beautiful as Your smile,and as beautiful as the Light of Your eyes.
And the Light of Your eyes, the Love of Your Heart causes my
heart to shine.
Thank You for Your Smile.

Is It True

GOD are You there? i heard about You, i heard about a way.
I heard about someone called "JESUS." I come to You with a
tear upon my heart.
I'm great, i'm weak
I'm beautiful, i'm ugly
I'm rich, i'm poor
I'm happy, i'm sad, I'm lost," i'm here."
Are You real, can i feel You, can i trust You, draw me close to
You.
GOD are You there? i heard about You, i heard about how Your
heart was a heart of mercy.
In a world that shows so very little mercy i heard about You, i
heard about someone called Jesus.
They said He was Your Son, they said i can trust Him, is it true?
can it be true?
In a world of so much pain, sorrow and suffering could there
still be hope?
They say "You are the true Light that changes not" and that
"You wipe away all tears,"
in a world of so many tears and so much darkness
can this be true?
I come to You with a tear upon my heart.
GOD are You there, is it true, can i hope?
It's been a long road and not always a straight one either, but
they said You were always near, is it true, were You always near?
ALWAYS?
Then You know where i've been and You know my mistakes, my
failures and my heart yet You can still love someone like me, this
is hard for me to understand.
They said "Wherever You have been, wherever You are now,
wherever You will go that You are Holy," but i am not,
i'm just me.

I'm great, i'm weak
I'm beautiful, i'm ugly
I'm rich, i'm poor, I'm happy, i'm sad,
I'm lost, --i'm here.
I come to You with a tear upon my heart.

Spring Time

In a world of so many bright lights and colors, so many different
flavors to taste, so many different ways to walk.
A million stop lights, a million one way only signs, a million
dead ends, a million dreams with many more broken.
Stay alert, keep your eyes wide open,
with my eyes wide open i didn't realize then how closed
they really were.
In a world where i drive 80 mph to work and back everyday, or
was it 800 mph, i forget.
Putting up with all the busy signals and all the noise pollution,
thru the maze of stop lights and the do not enter signs, with all
the traffic blocking my way everyday always slowing me down,
where was it again we were all going?
Was this a mistake in my mind or heart, i don't think so.
If we are so busy holding on to business what about our loved
ones? but i was making this drive because of my loved ones.
How quickly springtime passes, how quickly springtime goes by,
did i let it pass by too easy, did i not grasp it and hold it close
enough, was it because of summer thoughts or because spring
time comes every year.
Somehow, somewhere i learned to look at temporary things as
permanent, this can be a big mistake, and in seeing temporary
things as permanent did it cause me to hold them tighter or not
to hold them tight enough?
With my eyes wide open i didn't realize how much
i was not seeing.
I remember a time not long ago it was springtime, i stopped
listening to the music that i loved, time passed with no music,
and i really loved the music but i let it go, i chose because i was
lost in the storms and valleys of this world, and i came to realize
there was no love except one love that could save me. The Love
of the Holy Ones.
I needed to be re-aligned to Their love or it was the end.

I remember a time not long ago it was springtime,
a time for new beginnings.
GOD let the sweetest music of His heart go for a short time
to save what seemed to be permanent but what was really only
temporary and lost, to re-align His children back to Him,
Back to Life, Back to springtime forever. Thank YOU JESUS.

A Love That Would Never Let Go

The pressure of the bills i have to pay along with the chains that
i drag are all much weight upon my heart. To let my children go
out into this world from my sight, from my side,
oh my, help me Lord.
To get older and wonder who will be there to care for you or
even if you will have a place to live,
someplace warm when its cold out, someplace
safe in these times.
I didn't know a heart that carried so much weight and heaviness
could shake so easy.
Sometimes i feel like i'm being measured, i think i'm failing, to
often i go to bed depressed and i wake up angry or just tired. I
guess i didn't realize or have a clue about the seriousness of Your
love, a love that would never let go.
I run to You My GOD, i return to You, i will not be moved even
with all the bad news in the air.
I am not alone even when no one else is near, i will not give up,
i will remember You, i will stand fast in this storm. Your Holy
Love does hold me, the road ahead looks scary, the world is
shaking and turning, so much bad news and sorrow, but in Your
word You said it would be like this.
You saw all this even before it happened and You said "You
would never leave us, NEVER"
and You said "You would always be with us, ALWAYS."
In my heart, in my thoughts before, i needed to know what
"small" was so i could understand what "great'" was and i needed
to know what "beauty" was so i could understand
what "ugly" was.
So i thought and pictured in my mind "Beauty in the flesh, ugly
in the flesh," "Great in possession, nothing in possession."
Could a mirror reflect beauty? Could it weigh in
truth Beauty and Riches?
I think not the mirrors made by man, no, not the mirrors made
by man's hands, but i think the mirror in the sky can, the mirror

that separates the heavens from the earth, the mirror the Holy
Ones look through, and what do you think they see?
In the Cities in the East, In the Cities in the West,
In the Mountains in the North, In the Mountains in the South,
Among the Rich, Among the Poor,
Among the Happy, Among the Sad,
what do you think They see?
They see "Good and Bad, Right and Wrong, Fair and Unfair,
Just and Unjust."
Now i understand ; They see beauty in the flesh, They see ugly
in the flesh, They see great in possession, They see nothing in
possession because They are looking at the person's heart.
To be small and safe before Your Holy Throne and to be seen
as beautiful in Your eyes by Your Love is far better without
compare then to be beautiful and great in riches in this world.
I guess i didn't realize or have a clue about the seriousness
of Your Love.
A LOVE THAT WOULD NEVER LET GO.

On This Day

I woke up this morning tired, a full nights rest but still tired,
tired because my heart was heavy.
Maybe i just needed to help someone or maybe i just needed
someone to help me. Couldn't see any good i could do on this
day, me being well, just me.
I only change the calendar twice a year anymore, once in april,
once again at the end of december, i used to change it every
month, guess i just kinda gave up on it, you know, kinda just let
it go, things like that happen in this world. Thank You for april
and december, they see me through.
Reminds me of the time my wipers broke during an ice storm,
couldn't see anything, everything was cold and icy, the car was
going in any direction it wanted to, there wasn't even a safe place
to stop, it was pretty scary. It kinda felt like "what's going on" or
"why did they have to break now" or "not again, why me"?
Going through the day broken with no song to sing in my heart,
i think all the songs flew away,
"they found a warmer place to stay". Spinning, spinning,
spinning but getting nowhere, i think i could have made more
progress in neutral.
A short time back me and my friends gave a gift for Christmas
to a young lady alone with two sons, a couple weeks later we
gave her a small gift coupon for food.
On this day that i woke up tired, on this day my heart was
heavy, on this day of feeling i had nothing good to share, on this
day my wipers still broken because of the ice storm, a note was
given to me through a friend from the young lady alone with
two sons and it said;
Dear sir, thank you for your kindness and generosity, you helped
me and i'm a total stranger,
i'm trying to deal with everything in this world and i've never
been so scared in my life, but we are taking one day at a time.
Your kindness has helped my heart so, it inspires me to keep
going in a positive direction, thank you, signed Susan.

And i thought, you know it's the same way the Holy Ones move in my life, sometimes i feel so alone but i know They are always near, and when my wipers broke in that ice storm, when everything was so cold and i couldn't see and it was all so very scary. They brought me through, all the way through. When i couldn't see They saw for me, when i had no control, my heart finds peace knowing they are in control and i know what caused me to share on that day not long ago, it was the Love of the Holy Ones moving in my heart inspiring me to share, to give, to help, trying to be a reflection of what They have done and are doing in my life.

Well i got my wipers fixed but i'm still working on the calendar. Thank You My Lord GOD for Your Love. Thank You for april and december.

Thank You for JESUS.

ON THIS DAY AND EVERYDAY

Tears

Here i am it's another day, the ground is frozen and covered with snow, it's just getting light out and it's almost time to start work, man, i don't want to go out there again, i'm tired of freezing.
It's 20 degrees and all my tools are frozen and it feels more like minus ten.
It's hard to walk, just try to stay warm if you can, seasons will change the cold will go away,
in fifteen to twenty minutes my fingers will be froze then i'll have to go inside to get warm again,
"it's cold outside let me in."
There's a word i need to understand, i don't know why but it's stuck in my mind,
the word is "tears".
But before that let me introduce myself, welcome, "my name is bitterness," made bitter through the years of tears and struggle, who are you? sit if you have a moment.
And again, Hello, "my name is i don't care anymore," i gave up over the years, i'm tired of being tired, who are you? stay for a moment if you can.
And do you remember me? i am, "one who has a tear upon his heart," remember "behind the painted smile." Do you need to know my Christian name or does it matter?
And so now, there's a word i need to understand, the word is "tears."
Tears—they flow from the heart and go to the eye, i wonder why they come from the heart,
i wonder why they even are. What if i made my heart as cold as a stone, i wonder if your heart is
cold and dry if it can cry? Maybe it can just cry inside because it doesn't have enough tears to make it to the eye, i wonder if this could be seen as strength or maybe its just sad.
In the movies i remember a story where the person only cried "one tear, only one" and it ran down the side of their face slowly and that one tear made a million hearts to cry, why?

"Tears of pain, tears of sorrow" "Tears of joy, tears of happiness."
Tears of pain are bad they can hurt so very much. You Can Wipe
Them Off Your Face But You Can Not Wipe
Them Off Your Heart.
And it takes much time to heal a heart in pain, it's like the
passing of a storm. What is it that time possesses to be able to
heal a wounded heart, could it be Love?
Tears of Joy are good they give strength and energy. You Can
Wipe Them Off Your Face But A Smile Still Remains, Tears of
Joy are good.
Did the tears of joy have all that much more love in their lives
then did the wounded hearts, and then did the wounded hearts
have all that much less love and hope in their lives. I wonder
why the tears fall like they do? a few to some and more to others,
was it because of who deserved what? i don't think so. It's almost
like i can hear the hearts of pain crying and it sounds like;
"it's cold outside let me in, let me in. Why is all this pain cast on
me? It's cold outside let me in,
i need to be warm, i need to be warm,
it's cold outside let me in."
Friends try to heal and comfort, friends try to help, and friends
will even cry with you by your side,
and their hearts can really hurt to when they see your pain, but
only one love can touch a deeply wounded heart. It seems there's
not enough candles in the world to make all the tears of pain go
away, but i know it only takes one Light, one Love.
Only one Love can heal a heart that's crying, a hearts that's
dying, a heart that's been torn,
a heart that's been wounded even unto it's very soul,
it has to be a Holy Love.
I think to name my heart you can just call me "bitterness," and
it's me "i just don't care anymore," and do you remember me "i
come to you with a tear upon my heart,"
i need to get warm, to get warm.
Seasons will change, the cold will go away, the storm will pass.
I'll keep trying to hold on and if my grip slips i know in my soul
who holds me. My heart is cold, it feels like 20 degrees, no, it
feels more like minus ten. If this was a movie i'd turn the station

or walk out, if this was a story i'd find a happier one but its real
and it hurts, help me bear this weight.
"Upon Your Love i want to fly, Upon Your Love i need to soar,
but here i am,
so now within Your Love i need to hide, hide me, hide me deep
within Your Love where i can be alone, i need a place and time
to heal, i need to be alone, alone with You,
oh so deep inside Your Heart My GOD."
While i'm crying these tears i do not know where this path leads
that i cry from, but i know The One's who wipe all tears away.
Tears from a baby all the way to the tears of the old and all the
many rivers in between.
Tears from the beginning all the way to the tears of the end and
all the many faces in between.
You have been faithful my LORD and i am not even worthy of
Your Love.
Well my fingers are frozen and it's time to get warm "it's cold
outside, let me in."

Friend

It's morning time, i'm ready to lose again today, what's the use?
here i am in this pit and still trying to escape all the time falling
farther and farther down.
It's hard to sleep, it's hard to rest, it's hard to wake up and start
the day without caring, it's not something that we are taught
from the time that we are babes, no, were taught to keep trying.
It's hard when you know you are going to fail again today.
I have a question to ask You about "Light and dark and time,"
it can't be asked on high time but only in the morning time.
Strong coffee and a clear mind and then "the wonder why" will
take a walk without us "Friend."
Alcohol was a friend of mine, it proved itself many times, i
didn't find it, it found me, wasn't that my lucky day. It woke me
up and tucked me in, we walked together day to day, then it led
me to another one, another friend unto the end,
me, alcohol and drugs, among three friends,
made a pact unto the end.
And now it's the end and i'm here all alone, wasted life and
wasted time, those who said they were my friends were only
speaking lies. When all the mask are pulled away and all the
lies are exposed in truth, they were just using and abusing you,
calling you friend.
It's the end of the road and i'm not alone, there's a million
friends here with me both young and old, we had the same
guides, you know, "friends to the end," they'll tear you down
and break you, then chain you after your down. Drugs and
alcohol were a friend of mine, but here i am, burned out, beat
down, wiped out. Everything's a mess, that's me, just one big
mess, this is far past soap and water and comb your hair. In a
world of technology and all the many flavors, my heart needs
water and not from this world.
What happened, what went wrong, how far down is down? I
take one look at myself and my heart takes a dive, with tears or
without, an out of control dive down, all the way down.

How come there is no bottom in this pit, why, why, why?
In this pit, all alone, in the dark by myself, i saw a light, a
thousand lights shining bright upon the wall, all shining to catch
the eye of my heart, calling and speaking pleasant to me, saying
follow me it will be good.
Then i woke up in this pit, all alone by myself, all the the lights
were gone but "ONE,"
i was cold and scared and all alone, shaking in the dark.
Tell me why? Tell me why again they call this life? so many pits,
valleys and broken hearts.
I don't need any poems, rhymes,
or fancy words to finish this paper.
The Holy GOD sent His Holy Son to save me from this pit,
thank You JESUS.
It's morning time, i'm ready to try again today.

It's Time

Running out of my schedule, failing all the deadlines, failing,
but still on time, "lost time."
Chest hurts, side hurts, no time to let up yet. Down the road
aways maybe there will be time for me to catch my breath,
to reflect,to connect.
What happened to last time it was time for me to catch my
breath, to reflect, or maybe disconnect from life for a while? wait
a second, "last time" never showed up.
Bodies tired, it feels like war, it breaths one more sigh
in my self made sad.
Running in my schedule, meeting all the deadlines,
on top, but still on time, "lost time,"
chest hurts, side hurts, no time to let up yet, deflect the pain,
neglect yourself, my bodies blowing circuit breakers everyday.
Turn the key, plug me in, start me up, push me in the direction
that i need to be. Going in, going out, going here, going
there,going, going,going, GONE.
I need to lose this speed, i need to lose it now, but everytime i
touch the brakes i lose control.
I need to lose this speed, i need to lose it now, to take some time
to heal old wounds, to take some time to make up time,to take
some time to find the Light again.
To look outside, to look inside, to close my eyes, to identify,
to be real "Still."
BUT FIRST I HAVE TO GO, I HAVE TO GO FAST AND I
HAVE TO KEEP GOING,
i can't go slow, i have to keep going.
I'm going so fast my memory can't catch me, i'm going so fast
my imagination has left me,
i'm going so fast that dreams can't find me,
take time for this, take time for that,take time for this, take time
for that, take time for this, take time for that, and still on time,
"Lost time."

I need to lose this speed, i need to lose it now but everytime i touch the brakes i lose control.

Right now it's about going 90 mph, you know, 20 over the speed limit, sunup to sundown.

I'm at the point it needs to be done. It's time to make some decisions, it's something my hearts been struggling with for sometime now. There's times when making decisions you can get counsel from your friends, but there's times you can't listen to anyone, certain decisions you have to give it all to GOD, say your prayers, seek His Wisdom, then stand strong knowing in your heart and mind it's right.

It's Time To Lose This Speed, It's Time to Hit The Brakes And Hold On Tight.

Missing You

I lost a brother to cancer a few years ago, my mom left to be with him back in new york and stayed there two months, even at the point of sleeping in a chair at night by his bedside. When he died she came home. My one nephew who is very close to his grandma and who missed her so very much wrote his thoughts on a piece of paper and this is what it said, these are the words of a ten year old boy.

Dear grandma, i missed you alot. I know you've been through so much these past few weeks so we are going to try to make it up to you. We love you very much and don't want to see you sad. I hope this letter will cheer you up. For Christmas we didn't even have a Christmas tree but that is not the point. What i am trying to say is the holidays weren't the same without you. But we know you needed to be with uncle paul and we know he needed you there with him.

Even willie the cat was smelling all over the place trying to figure out where you were, he was worried you would not come back home to.

The holidays will never be the same without you. I know you can get through this and i know we can all get through this together. When you came back i was so happy, that is why i couldn't stop talking. When i got you back my very, very special friend i felt the best feeling i have ever had, i hope you never go away again.

On the way to new york we didn't have fun at all. All we had to do was listen to our cd player and play games on hunters cell phone, we ran out of batteries on both the cell phone and the cd player, but when we got there it was worth it, when i got to see you grandma and grandpa.

I got you that vanilla candle, i knew that candle was for you. The other vanilla candles you would not have liked they didn't smell good enough. I only buy the best things for the best people and that includes you. You are unbelievable, you have no idea how much i love you.

Willie the cat sits for hours waiting for mice to come through the back door but we had to wait for weeks to see you walk through the door back to us. THE END.

The boy's name is craig and hunter is his older brother. Brother Paul is home in heaven before us.

Gifts of Heartache

Gifts of heartache they bring to me, across the miles,
from far away
Saying, hold me in Your arms, hold me in Your arms,
hold me in Your arms My God, My King
Gifts of heartache they look so tired,
i see their beauty beyond their tears,
it's a desert in their hearts, searching in the wind,
staring at the sky, trouble all around.
Gifts of heartache they bring to me, they walk the
valley of suffering,
losing hope as time goes by, bitten with despair,
Saying hold me in Your arms My God, My King.
Gifts of heartache they bring to me, little candles
who lost their way,
saying how can we go on, it's getting harder everyday,
i need to fall into Your arms My God, My King,
saying how can we go on, it's getting harder everyday,
i need to fall into Your arms, to be lost inside Your love.
Gifts of heartache they bring to Him, among
their faces i see myself,
broken and alone, trying to go on, needing to be held,
falling to the ground.
The joy of Heaven is graced to me,
God's Holy Son bearing tender mercies,
sweet, sweet mercies,sweet, sweet mercies, sweet sweet mercies,
Holy Love from above.
Heal my brokenness, make me strong again,
please never leave my side, no,seal me with Your kiss,
heal my brokenness, make me strong again,
please never leave my side love, seal me with Your kiss.
Holy Holy is Your love,

Holy Holy is Your love, i need to fall into Your arms, to be lost
inside Your love.
Lost inside Your love is the dream inside of me,
the dream inside of me is to be lost inside Your love.
Mathew chpt. 9 vs 36

Jesus is the Way

Enter in to pain and sorrow King,
come into my life and what remains,
The pain it cuts so deep i cannot speak,
make this time to pass, just go away.
So far away from me i feel so weak,
the sun still shines today but not for me.
I hang my head and cry, i feel so cold,
something in me died, it went away.
Locked safe inside my heart it was called love,
their face and name remains but not their touch.
Their voice and words they spoke i hold on to,
i pray it was just a dream and i'd awake.
I'd pull you close to me and say how much,
i love your everything, i love your love,
You brought color to my life and sunshine to,
your a blessing from above, a friend so true.
Take my love away with you, may it keep you warm,
never say goodbye, it's not the end.
Jesus is the way, the way back home, the words He spoke are
true, we're not alone.
They'll take away the pain and suffering.
Loved ones you cry for now you'll see again.
Jesus is the way, the way back home, the words He spoke are
true, we're not alone.
They'll take away the pain and suffering.
Loved ones you cry for now you'll see again.
Hebrews chpt. 2 vs 14 & 15

Treasures in a Field

Mathew Chpt. 13 vs 44. King James Version
"Again, the kingdom of heaven is like unto treasure hid in a
field; the which when a man
has found; he hides, and for joy thereof goes and sells all that he
has, and buys that field."

The teacher asked the student what do you understand about
this verse, the student said i understand that the treasure hid in
the field is the word of God and the love of God. The teacher
said this is good but now look at it again but this time picture
it in your mind and tell me what you see. The student says i
see a man going through a field and he finds the word of God
and it is a treasure to him, it's good in his heart and he needs
to have it, so he sells all that he has so he can buy the field and
keep this treasure. The teacher said this is good but now i want
you to send two men through the field, have one joy in finding
the treasure and the other man not. Picture it in your mind and
tell me what you see. Student says, o.k. the first man goes into
the field and finds this treasure and it's good in his heart and
he needs to have it. Now here goes the second man and he sees
the same treasure but says, this is a treasure for you but it is not
a treasure for me, it is not good in my heart. My treasures are
gold and silver, the desire of beautiful women, power, fame and
fortune, these are the treasures of my heart.

The teacher said, so now it seems that there is more than one
treasure in this field, so this is what we will do, we'll take the
treasure of the word of God and set it to the right in the field.
Then we will take all the other treasures, the gold and silver and
all the rest of them and put them in one group and we will call
the group "the treasures of the world," then we will set them to
the left in the field. Now i want you to send them through again
but this time instead of two different men i want you to send
two separate groups of people. Let one group be drawn straight
to the treasure of the word of God and the other group to the

treasures of the world. Picture it in your mind and tell me what you see. The student says, there they go, one group is being drawn to the right, to the treasure of God's love and the other group is being drawn to the left, to the treasures of the world. The teacher pauses for a few seconds to see what the student has learned, but the student is quiet. The teacher says lets do this one more time. We will keep the two separate treasures in the field the same but this time we're going to take the two separate groups of people and mix them all together. Now send them through the field and tell me what you see. There's a look of interest on the students face now as he gets ready to send them through. The student now is picturing this multitude of people going forward, a vast multitude pressing forward through this field. Up and to the right he sees the treasure of God's love and over to the left he sees the treasures of the world. The teacher says again tell me what you see. The student says, i see them going forward, some are being drawn to the right and some are being drawn to the left. Their being drawn to the right, their being drawn to the left. Their being separated, their being separated. Many are being drawn to the love of God and the others are being drawn to the treasures of the world. Their being separated, there's a separation taking place.

And in that moment it was like you could see the light of understanding shining on the students face as he said, i understand now, the people are being separated, the field is not just a field, no, it's the earth and this walk through the field is them living their lives upon this earth.

The teacher said you've come along ways young man but i have a question for you. If the word of God is so vital to be needed why does it say, "that the treasure was hid in the field?"

This is the answer that i got. Walk into a room full of candles and light one candle for the treasure of God's love. Now in that same room light another candle for gold,and light another candle for power,and another candle for desiring beautiful women, and another candle for fame, and another candle to own titles and deeds. Light a candle in that room for every single

treasure of the world, and now you have a room filled with candles shining.
Now tell me which candle is the treasure of God's love? you cannot, because it now appears to be hid among all the other lights shining all around it.
So how Do You know which one it is?

⚜

The Mustard Seed

Mathew Chpt.13 vs 31-32, King James Version
"The kingdom of heaven is like to a grain of mustard seed,
which a man took, and sowed in his field. Which indeed is the
least of all seeds, but when it is grown, it is the greatest among
herbs, and becomes a tree, so that the birds of the air come and
lodge in the branches thereof."
The teacher asked the student what do you understand of this
teaching.? The student said, i don't really have a clue of what
it means. I only know a little about mustard and herbs, i don't
understand, why doesn't it say something like, "the kingdom of
heaven is like unto a great oak tree, strong and true."
The teacher said that's interesting but let us continue, i want you
to take that tiny mustard seed and plant it and tell me what you
see in your mind. So the student takes the seed and he plants it
and watches it grow into a plant, but his mind is still empty.
The teacher says, do it again. So the student tries again, he takes
the seed in his fingers, plants it, and watches this plant grow into
the greatest of herbs plus also a tree, but this time thoughts and
questions come into his mind.
This mustard seed is not only a herb but it
becomes the greatest of herbs, plus also a tree.
Question, no other seed among the whole
herb family can do this,?
Answer, no, no other seed among the whole
herb family can do this.
Question, no other seed among the whole tree
family can do this.?
Answer, no, no other seed among the whole
tree family can do this.
Student replies, so this seed, and only this one seed, can become
the greatest of herbs plus a tree also, interesting. That makes this
seed separate, special, unique because no other seeds can do this.
It's like it can cross over between the herb family
and the tree family.

It's like it can cross over between the two families, it can break down barriers between them, it can unite the two families together. The teacher says continue.

It can cross over, it can unite, it can break down barriers, it can cross over, it can cross over, it can cross over, wait
---------------- "who crossed over"?

Then the student said, i understand now, Jesus Christ crossed over. He's the only one who can say, "I am the Son of The Living God yet I was also a man of flesh who walked upon this earth." Uniting the family of man back with the family of GOD.

A 5 Dollar Testimony

A while back i went up to the local fast food drive in for lunch.

While i was there a friend pulled in a few stalls away, she's always been a nice lady to me, so when she saw me she just smiled and waved. While i was waiting for my order to be delivered this thought came to me, "you know, it would be a good idea to buy her lunch for her without her knowing," i'll just drive away and see her down the road later on.

Well, time had passed and one day i pulled into the grocery store parking lot and there was this sweet Christian lady. She saw me and walked directly to me. With eyes of compassion and a voice shaking a tiny bit she said, michael, i just wanted to thank you so very much, i was having one of the worst days of my life and when you shared that small kindness to me it changed everything, it really, really helped my heart so much.

When she told me it was one of the worst days of her life she really meant it. I do not know if it was because of her daughters joining the military and heading to the Middle East or not, i didn't need to know, but what i can tell you is, before she walked away she smiled the most beautiful smile towards me.

The good Lord has taught me how powerful small acts of kindness can be, time and time again.

It was less than five dollars and look at the impact it had.

Well, now it's today and I'm getting ready to head up street, guess what I'm going to do.

Printed in the United States
By Bookmasters